T0082927

Godly
Tendecies 2

ALAN HINES

Order this book online at www.trafford.com
or email orders@trafford.com

Most Trafford titles are also available at major online book retailers.

© Copyright 2021 Alan Hines.
All rights reserved. No part of this publication may be reproduced, stored in a retrieval
system, or transmitted, in any form or by any means, electronic, mechanical, photocopying,
recording, or otherwise, without the written prior permission of the author.

Print information available on the last page.

ISBN: 978-1-6987-0711-2 (sc)
ISBN: 978-1-6987-0712-9 (hc)
ISBN: 978-1-6987-0710-5 (e)

Because of the dynamic nature of the Internet, any web addresses or links contained in
this book may have changed since publication and may no longer be valid. The views
expressed in this work are solely those of the author and do not necessarily reflect the
views of the publisher, and the publisher hereby disclaims any responsibility for them.

Any people depicted in stock imagery provided by Getty Images are models, and such
images are being used for illustrative purposes only.
Certain stock imagery © Getty Images.

Trafford rev. 04/27/2021

www.trafford.com
North America & international
toll-free: 844-688-6899 (USA & Canada)
fax: 812 355 4082

BOOKS OF POETRY ALREADY PUBLISHED BY ALAN HINES,

1. Reflections of Love
2. Thug Poetry Volume 1
3. The Words I Spoke
4. Joyce
5. Constant Visions
6. Red Ink of Blood
7. Beauty of Love
8. Reflections of Love Volume 2
9. Reflections of Love Volume 3
10. True Love Poetry
11. Visionary.
12. Love Volume 1
13. This is Love
14. Garden of Love
15. Reflections of Love Volume 4
16. Reflections of Love Volume 5
17. Reflections of Love Volume 6
18. Reflections of Love Volume 7
19. Reflections of Love Volume 8
20. Reflections of Love Volume 9
21. Reflections of Love Volume 10
22. Godly Tendencies
23. Admiration of Love
24. Admiration of Love Volume 2

URBAN NOVEL ALREADY PUBLISHED BY ALAN HINES,

1. Book Writer
2. Queen of Queens
3. Lost in a Poet Storm

1. Reflections of Love Volume 3
2. This is Love (Volume 1, 2, and 3)
3. Founded Love (Volume 1, 2, and 3)
4. True Love (Volume 1, 2, and 3)
5. Love (Endless Volumes)
6. Tormented Tears (Volume 1, 2, and 3)
7. A Inner Soul That Cried (Volume 1, 2, and 3)
8. A Seed That Grew (Volume 1, 2, and, 3)
9. The Words I Spoke (Volume 2, and 3)
10. Scriptures (Volume 1, 2, and 3)
11. Revelations (volume 1, 2, and 3)
12. Destiny (Volume 1, 2, and 3)
13. Trials and Tribulations (Volume 1, 2, and 3)
14. IMMORTALITY (Volume 1,2, and 3)
15. My Low Spoken Words (Volume 1, 2, and 3)
16. Beauty Within (Volume 1, 2, and 3)
17. Red Ink of Blood (Volume 1, 2, and 3)
18. Destiny of Light (Jean Hines) (Volume 1, 2, and 3)
19. Deep Within (Volume 1, 2, and 3)
20. Literature (Volume 1, 2, and 3)
21. Silent Mind (Volume 1, 2, and 3)
22. Amor (Volume 1, 2, and 3)
23. Joyce (Volume 1, 2, and 3)
24. Lovely Joyce (Volume 1, 2, and 3)
25. Pink Lady (Volume 1, 2, and 3)
26. Mockingbird Lady (Volume 1, 2, and 3)
27. Enchanting Arrays (Volume 1, 2, and 3)
28. Harmony (Volume 1, 2, and 3)
29. Realism (Volume 1, 2, and 3)
30. Manifested Deep Thoughts (Volume 1, 2, and 3)
31. Poectic Lines of Scrimage (Volume 1, 2, and 3)
32. Garden of Love (Volume 1, 2, and 3)
33. Reflection In The Mirror. (Volume 1, 2, and 3)

Upcoming non-fiction books by Alan Hines,

1. Time Versus Life
2. Timeless Jewels
3. The Essence of Time
4. Memoirs of My Life
5. In my Eyes To See
6. A Prisoner's Black History

Upcoming Urban Novels by Alan Hines,

1. Black Kings
2. Playerlistic
3. The Police
4. Scandalous Scandal
5. The West Side Rapist
6. Shattered Dreams
7. She Wrote Murder
8. Black Fonz
9. A Slow Form of Suicide
10. No Motherfucking Love
11. War Stories
12. Ghetto Heros
13. Boss Pimps
14. Adolescents
15. In The Hearts of Men
16. Story Teller
17. Kidnapping
18. Mob Ties

ACKNOWLEDGEMENTS

Heavenly Father thank you for blessing me to live to see another day; thank you for all your many blessings which include me writing and being able to publish another book.

1. I WONDER

I wonder when will you be coming back to claim the souls of
your kids upon Earth.
Those that was buried up under the dirt now shall
see paradise of your finest works.
For sins of adults children wont be cursed.
At funerals those tears shall become joy as we meet up
as family reunion of no more pain,
for the best better, instead of worse.
A divine majesty for those that
studied and obeyed the word.
Seeds of eternity souls of Africans,
middle passage traveled turned slaves shall be
free above the clouds beyond the Earth.
Family, friends, and enemies shall be together
as angels of one, one accord of our Father
whom are in Heavens work.

2. PURPOSELY PLAN

A purpose, a plan.
Lord knows, holds us up
to withstand.

3. SHE WAS

She was the light that shined.
She was that tall mountain I was willing to climb.
She was so sweet, she'd even bring forth
a natural sweetner in a lime.
Bless the day the Lord made her mines.

4. ORCHESTRATE

Our Lord of Lords,
our king of kings,
please continue to be our saviour
for us orchestrate things.
In the darkness be that gleam.
Let us not go astray but lead us into
beautiful things.

5. INVENTOR OF LIFE

The inventor of itself life.
The only God that could impregnant
a woman without intercourse, Joseph's wife.
The one that loves as his kids that after
life he gives their souls eternal life
with him in paradise.

6. WILL

Will, and might.
Gift, and sight.
High of life.
The love of life.
Pray to him but only through Christ.

7. HEAVEN KNOWS

Heaven only knows.
Lord knows.
Follow his path
as a seed to grow.

8. REFLECTION OF GOD

Be a reflection of him,
and be great.
Always pray for better days.
His sun shine always shine
before, and after a rainy day.

9. CROWN

The drums are heard,
as the trumpets sound.
The melodies are soothing and
and floats around.
Only God shall wear the crown.

10. FAITHFUL SERVANT

For I am a servant of the Lord,
in the sanctified non violent army of the Lord.
One accord.
For him I worship I adore.
No one but God I shall fear,
no other God I shall worship
or try to restore.
Faithful servant love you, amor.

11. TESTIMONY

Testimony: Would never leave me lonely.
Genuine the one and only.
The inventor of time,
father time, the one and only.

I never knew that once a upon
a time in America I couldn't
even write a letter now I write music,
and poetry as a trendsetter,
love of life that couldn't get better.

Freedom that rang, I had a dream.
An African king.

I always had love in which came from
Heaven's Above.

12. LADY LADY DISGUISE

Lady without disguise.
The one I wanna see each morning as open my eyes.
You be my daylight, my sunrise.
You be a winner, trophie, prize.
You be the love I need, cherish worship,
to to rely.

A love, lady love without disguise.

13. HOLY GHOST

Coasting.
Praising God Holy Ghosting.

Free.
Free to roam the Earth
reading the scriptures of time,
making love to your mind.
Endless in time.
Love, divine.
King of Kings,
Lord of Lords,
Ruler of mankind.

14. WE SHALL

We shall shine.
We shall be free.

We shall faithfully worship God.
We shall live throughout eternity.

We shall embrace the wind that blow
as the essence of time,
in mind, we shall shine.

15. SOULMATE

Soulmate love in each and everyway.
A sunshine of enchanting arrays.
Love without delay.
Special as birth, born again life
within the coming of days.

Soulmate together until our last days.

16. FOREVER, AND EVER

Forever.
And ever.
Love that didn't get better.
A Rose a feather.
Love together forever.

Forever.
And ever.

17. TO COME ALIVE

To come alive.
To be free from sinful ties.
To be baptize.
To see the sunrise within her eyes.
To live, to be alive.

18. SHE WAS

She.
She was a jewel.

She.
She was a collectors item a keeper.

She.
She was love,
love that didn't get any deeper.

19. IN SPACE

In space,
in time,
love to my mind.
Love multiplied as peace
a thousand times.

In space,
in time,
you shall be mines.

In space in time,
mountains we climb.

20. HER STYLE

Her style.
Her smile.

Her love.
Her joy.

Her caress.
Her heart, mind,
and flesh.

21. NO REGRETS

Whenever,
however,
to feel the affect.
Love without reject.
Confess.
No upsets.
Loving at it's best.
And yes I have no regrets.

22. CAME

Came.
Pleasure aimed.

Came.
To ease brains.

Came.
I shall forever glorify,
thou name.

23. WHAT WE CAN'T SEE

What we can't see and touch,
love in it's abundance as much.

We can't even imagine across the lines
of scrimage but your love is free from blemish.

We love very much, in him, in God we trust.

24. LOVE, LOYALTY

Love.
Loyalty.
Royalty.

25. LOVE IN EXISTENCE

The meaning the definition.
Love within existence.
Love that's relentless.
Love from a vast distance.
Love in existence.

26. DEPEND

Don't depend on your own understanding.
Love which is outstanding.
Love to forever be in demanding.
Never knew what the future has in store,
from the man upstairs in which we're depending.....

27. CHAPELS OF

Chapels of love in mind.
That of the creators will, and design.
Love all the time.

28. THE DAYS

The days of summer.
A love like no other.

The days of spring.
I glorify, and sing.

The days of our lifetime.
Together we live together we shine.

29. THE WAY

The way we live,
lovely throughout years.

The way we float,
loves overdose.

The way we be,
anxious, willing, free.

30. IN TIME OF ROMANCE

In time of romance,
love withstand.

In times of need,
your love be nutrition to feed,
wonderful deeds, fresh air we breathe.

In times of romance,
love together as we hold hands
to strip to dance.

31. EVER MORE

Ever more,
love I adore.

Ever be,
you and me.

Ever care,
love beyond compare.

32. LOVE, RESIDE

Love to forever reside.
Coincide.
Love to rely.
Love forever upon,
and below the friendly skies.
Loves enterprise.

33. DEPTH

In the depth of time.
Love to my mind.

In the depth of never ending,
love replenished.

In the depth of flesh,
love without a contest.

34. GLEAM, DREAM

Dream.
Gleam.
For your love I fiend.
My lady, my queen.
For you I'll
do anything.

35. SPIRITUAL GUIDANCE

Spiritual guidance,
love residing.

Spiritually inclined.
Holy, divine.

Spiritually sent.
A womanly prince.

36. BEHOLD

Behold the power of love,
the power of God.

Behold shape, format,
in the likeness of God,
God bless our souls.

Behold a love,
a joy formed.
Behold the essence of God
as going to him in the sky as you
ride a black Stallion, or a Unicorn.

37. SUNDAY SCHOOL

As a kid in Sunday school,
I never knew that this love
would've have growed, grew.
Melodies of a flute, love unto.
Brothers, and sisters of Christ
as one in the same of group.
Love unto.
The cross of time in which our sins
are forgiving unto.

38. PRIVILEGE

Thanks for being giving.
Forgiving.
Giving life to be living.
Thanks for being our father,
to us you are a privilege.

39. FATHER GOD

Father God beyond Mars.
Gratitude for your precious blessings thus far.

Father time forgive my sins,
ease my mind.

Father of more than the galaxy,
please make my dreams reality,
please continue to look over strangers,
so called friends, and family.

40. AT PEACE

At peace.
Crush Satan, Dragon of the beast.

At time.
Love all the time.

Within timely sessions of quest,
Heavenly father you are the best.

41. TAKE HEED TO

Take heed to scriptures.
Be a reflection of God daily
as you look in the mirror.
Visionary, visions as we float
through time as his words become clearer.

42. CALLED PARADISE

A place called paradise.
Soaring through the heights.
A hunger for love as an appetite.

43. A ESTATE

A great estate.
Love before, and beyond this present day.
Bow your head, as we get on our knees for prayer to pray.

44. GOAT

God is the true goat.

Good on all terms,
you live you learn.

Burning fire in the eyes to burn.

For your love we need, we yearn.
Never a dull moment each day within seconds
in turn to love us as you do firm.

Live and learn I bare witness to charities
of God in turn, live, learned, a shelter of
a palace and your seed in turn. The love of God
to forever more stand firm.

Love God, live, learn.

True number one Goat,
God is good on all terms.

45. SHE WAS MY DAILY

She was my daily shine.
My everyday Valentine.
Love at all times.
Made love to her soul, heart, mind.
Blessed to have her as mine.

46. LOVE WITHOUT ENDING

A new day.
A new beginning.
Everlasting love without ending.

47. OF A NEW BIRTH

Bring me the news of a new birth.
New life for what it's worth.

Bring to me the essence of time,
through will make love to my mind.

Bring the greatness of destiny to be,
an everlasting love for you, and me.

48. MENTION

Attention.
Honorable mention.
Love without resistence.

49. A BETTER WAY

A will a way.
Pray for better days.

A rhythm, a rhyme.
Pray all the time.

A rhyme, a reason,
pray throughout each seasons.

50. TRANSFORMATION

Lovely as the transformation
of a butterfly.

Lovely as the sunrise
upon the blue sky.

Lovely as the changing of time
the breeze of mines,
peace unto mankind.

51. IN HER I SEE

In her I see my future to be.
In her I see birth of a planted seed.
In her I see my love to be.
In her, she.

52. TRADE IN

Trade in my life for yours.
I adore, me amor.

Trade in my existence.
Love even from a vast distance.

Trade in my time,
love to shine, lovely, and divine.

53. WITHSTAND

To withstand.
Love grand.
Such a great romance.
Love to withstand.

54. TO BE CHERISHED

To be loved.
To be cherished.
To be love, cherished,
love and marriage.

55. GLIDE

The way you glide.

The way you speak,
melodies of love being reached.

The way you remain,
love gain.

56. ATTRACT

Attraction.
Great satisfaction.
Love everlasting.
The center of my heart's attraction.

57. I MUST

Quest.
Blessed.
I love God,
I must confess.

58. PLEASE BE

Please be mines.
Make love to my body,
and mind.

59. PURPOSE DRIVEN

Purpose driven.
An ancore of love giving.

Purpose and faith love,
as we visualize judgement day stepping
into the Pearly gates.

60. THEREFORE

There for.
Love galore.
To adore.
Love wanting more.

61. LOVE GREATER

Love greater.

Love shown.

Love from you is as a place called home.

62. I SHALL CLIMB

For you I shall climb mountains.

For you I shall swim through Oceans, Seas.

For you I shall be all I can be.

63. IT'S BEST

Best.
Caress.
Tenderness of time within Earthly
bodies of flesh.
Loving at it's best.

64. GLORIFY LOVE

Came.
Glorify thou name.

In the midst.
I never knew a love like this.

Within.
Love to contend.

65. WALK WITH ME

Walk with me.
Talk with me.
Lead me in the path righteousness.
God's child as I be your Godly seed.

66. ABOVE AVERAGE

Above average.
Lovable, and lavish.
Love defying.
Love undying.

Above average.

67. IN LOVE, IN TIME

In love.
In grace.
In time.
In quality, taste.

68. THE YEARS

The years of life we live.
Thanking you for blessing us to be here.
In God we trust and only in him we fear.
Love of life to always be near.

69. REJOICING

Rejoice.
Peoples choice.
Peaceful without noise.

Sing.
Celebrate.
Rejoice.

70. FLOURISHED GIFTS

To be loved.
To be felt.
To be encouraged.
To be with gifts flourished.

71. MAINTAIN

To maintain.
Love gained.
Remained.
Sweet as sugar cane.

72. GROWTH, PROSPER

Growth.
Prosper.
Enhance.
Stand tall, newly brand.

73. THANK YOU GOD

God thank you for blessing us to still be living.
Lovely as your children.

Thank you for another day down here on Earth.
Bless since birth.

Thank you for always being by our side,
a tour guide, a safety shell of love to coincide.

Thank you for paving the way down the road of life
to forever rely.

74. BECAUSE OF

Because I am happy, because I am free.
Because of the love within life you've giving me.

75. ETERNITY

Create clean spirit in me.
Love throughout eternity.
The only love anew in which I could see.
The love you is, is for me.

Love throughout eternity.

76. OF THE THROWN

King of the thrown.
Upon judgement day I shall meet
you when it's time to go home.
Love of our own.
Souls fly high to carry on.

77. THE JOY

I could tell the joy it would last forever.

If I could feel the vibe it would be endless pleasure.

If I could her voices it would be pleasant in decisional choices.

78. ETERNAL CIRCUMSTANCES

We can be that eternal circumstances of living.
Be great honor the law of God ten commandments of scriptures.
We can forever worship God while still living.

79. PERFORM

Perform.
Lovely a birth, the day we were born.

Remain.
Love one in the same.

Define.
Love on my mind.

80. OF COURSE

Of course.
On track, the right course.

A goal.
God please give me greatness, bless thou soul.

Achieve.
Lord, please walk by my side to never leave.

81. PREACH

Reach.
Teach.
Preach.

82. MESSAGE

Advance.
The changing time within circumstance.
To be grand.
To take a stand.
Cherish God, a message to each woman, and man.

83. FOR CONFESSION

Blessings.
Lessons.
No sins for confession.

84. LORD

Lord, each time I thought I couldn't make it,
love came without hesitation.

Lord, when I thought I couldn't succeed you were
there for me indeed.

When I needed a friend in prayer you was my friend to the end,
to always be there.

85. PROTEIN

Protein.
Love stream.
My everything.
Her and I king and queen.

86. ALPHA

Alpha, and Omega.
Love that couldn't get any greater.

Father of all things.
The one and only real king.

87. GOD OF LOVE

Was love.
Is love.
God of love.

88. GARDEN OF

Garden of love.
Garden of fruit.
Garden of Eden, love unto.

89. SUCH A CONNECTION

I feel such a connection.
Sense of protection.
Highest degree of affection.
Truly a blessing.

90. THE TOUCH, THE FEEL

The touch.
The feel.
The loving was really, real.

91. MY GOD

My God created the Earth, Moon, and stars.

My God liberate those confined freeing souls, and body parts.

My God is an awesome God, thus far.

92. TO DO

To do.
To Love.
To breathe.
To see.
Father in Heaven whom loves endlessly.

93. TIME FRAME

The time frame remains.
To put Lucifer to shame.
Happiness gained.
Lunch break is over it's time
to get back in church I hear the
church bells ring.
Let the chorus of Gospel sing.
Lord of lord, king of kings.

94. THE REASON

The reason why I live.
I know it's going to be some rainy days in which
I should shed tears.
But the love of God is still here.
In God we trust, and only in him we shall fear.

The reason why I was giving life to live.

95. OVATION

Wonferful.
Golden.

Gracious.
Ovation.

Lovely in all ocassions.

96. IN LOVE

In time.
In love.
In love with our Father
whom are in Heaven up above.

97. NOURISHMENT TO FEED

Dreamed.
Believed.
Achieved.
With aim to please.
God's love as nourishment to feed.

98. OF STONE

Houses built of stone.
Spirits of deceased ancenstors roam.
A love of our own.
A special place of love called home.
The lake shores of time in which the creator own.

99. AGAIN, AND AGAIN

Again, and again your love has no end.
The blood of your only begotten son, allows us to be forgiving for sins.
Lovely as the time within the waters in which fish swim.
Lovely as the healthy birth of twins.
Lovely as the days of joy without end.

100. TENDECIES

God's tendecies.
Loving plenty.
Surrounding by his invisible angles, many.
Love of God's tendecies.

PREVIOUS BOOK
OF POETRY PUBLISHED
BY
ALAN HINES

GODLY TENDENCIES

1. SING

I sing because I'm happy.
I sing because I'm free.
I sing because I love Jesus and his, our
father God and I know both loves me.

2. CHOOSE GOD FIRST

Choose God First.
Maintain visions of his sons rebirth.
Bless to still be living, breathing
down here on Earth.

3. REACH

Strength to reach heights peeks to succeed.
Love life vitality air in which we breathe your
divine seeds.
Covered by the blood of your only begotten
son forgiving us for all bad deeds.
Teach and lead.
Sorrows to bleed.

4. GOD GAVE

God gave my wisdom.
God gave me life.
God gave me courage.
God gave me a vision of sight.

5. BE SMART

Be smart.
Continue to work hard.
Shine a light ignite a flame
in the dark.
Let your love continue to flow
endlessly after it's initial
start.
Keep the faith keep believing in God.

6. LEARNING EXPERIENCES

Life is a learning experience learned from good and
bad lessons.
To be breathing still living is a mere blessing.
We must honor our father whom are in the Heavens.
Try our best to commit no sins for confessions.
Knowing with each one of our Earthly flesh we was born with
imperfections but we still contend to be the best
on the outside and within each lessons living life to fullest as
it is what it is a blessing.

7. GOD PUT A SMILE ON MY FACE

God put a smile on my face that can't be erased;
his eternal love mercy and grace.
I honor his name I shall never disgrace.
Faithful servant shall never go astray.
I pray that I shall meet him once my
Earthly flesh perishes away.

8. GREATFUL

Greatful for every blessing, Godly session, each learned lesson.
Love the aged and the young and the restless.
Covered by the blood of Jesus dressings,
still living breathing throughout the polluted air sinful messes.
Honor thou name even after death and
these are my confessions.

9. TIME OF ESSENSCE

Time is of essence.
Every experience good
or bad is a learn lesson.
Cherish life appreciate blessings.

10. DETERMINED

Determined.
Yearning.
Desire God instead of Lucifer's sinful burning.

11. THANKING GOD FOR LIVING

Soon It'll be Thanksgiving.
365 days I'm thanking God for living.
Admiration for each blessing giving.
Proud as one of his children.

12. GRATITUDE

Gratitude for all the things you have done and will do.
The love of life you gave to me unto.
Woke up today still breathing within life, true.
The Alpha the Omega Lord of Lords King of Kings guru.
The light of greatness the forever shines through.
Forever loyal unto you.
Lord of lords king of kings....guru....

13. TAKE YOUR TIME

Take your time.
Live life and shine.
Observe your surroundings never be in the blind.
Always make it better than the last time.

14. BLESSED TO BE LIVING

Bless to still be living.
Father watch over our seeds,
God bless the children.
No sad poems no tormented tears from stray bullets
of accidental senseless killings.
Know that you all are beautiful as God's children.
You deserve more than check to check living,
because you are worth millions.

15. YOU DESERVE

You deserve happiness instead of grief.
Love instead of beef.
Multiplication of peace.
Within vitality find a way of being free.

16. PRAISE

Praise thou holy name since he gave me birth
love in abundance became.
Pray each morning I awake no matter if it's
sunny or thundering rain.

17. GOD FIRST

Always choose God first.
Through prayer thank him for giving
you birth.
Love life to the fullest appreciating
each blessing for what it's worth.

18. THE LOVE OF GOD

Thanks for the love again, and again.

Lord I remember a time where I
didn't have anything thanks to
you I'm wealthy as a king.

I can remember a time when I was confined
know I'm free as can be thanks to thee.

I can remember a time being sick
now my health is fixed.

I can remember a time when I had no where
to live know I own buildings.
Blessings from God the love of life living.
Wonderful feelings.

Thanks for your love, again, and again my one
and only true friend.

19. GOOD

Good to people.
Loving as a sequel.
To God we're all
his children and should be treated as
an equal.

20. THANK GOD FOR BLESSINGS.

Thank God for his many blessings.
Lean on God not your own understanding
for less stressing.
Be blessed all through the decisional lessons.

Thank God for blessings.

21. LOVE IN ADVANCE

We praise you in adavance
love of life blessings in which it stands.
Please continue to watch our children
and even the adults women, and men.
Truly beautiful, truly grand.

Through love, and prayer we praise you
in advance.

22. THE LOVE OF

The love of
the love God.

The love spiritual guidance
we need and desire beyond mars.

The love of life, loyalty and
love from God always helps
us to get through, thus far.

23. GOD'S GRACE, AND MERCY

God's grace.
Loving that can't be replace.
Souls snatched up to be Heavenly placed.

24. PLEASE KEEP

Heavenly father keep blessing us down here on Earth.
Please continue to bless us, love us for what it's worth.
Praise our father whom are in Heaven in which gives us birth.

25. LORD OF LORDS.

Lord of Lords.
King of Kings
your love is everything.
As your sun ray of sunlights shine
we know that you are everything.
Life and love is what you bring.
Glorious father for you we sing.

Lord of Lords.
King of Kings.

26. SHE STUDIED

She studied the word of
Deuteronomy, Proverbs, and Psalms.
She'd preach the gospel of the Lord
that the judgement day was soon to come.
The Mayans time wasn't accurate but judgement
day was soon to come something we can't
run from.
Birds fly from palms of hands to worship
our father God whom are in Heaven kingdom to come.....
Deuteronomy, Proverbs, and Psalms.

27. ETERNAL WORLD

Eternal world without end.
Father forgive us for our sins,
through the son of man.
Lord allow your love to ever more
suspend.

Eternal love, eternal peace, eternal
life without end.

28. GODLY STYLE

Godly child.
Godly style.
Loving all the while.

29. PRAY

Pray for better.
Pray the shining star of the Lord shall
ever more shine your way.
Pray to receiving God's enchanting array.

Pray for better days pray.

30. SEVEN CANDLES

The seven candle sticks shall be cast to the seven churches.
Love, power shall be dispurse.

Worship, and honor.
Our father whom are in Heaven is marvelous.

Honor thou name regardless.

Printed in the United States
by Baker & Taylor Publisher Services